Managing Socially:
The Social Process Model

socialprocessmodel.com

by Elias Saad

With insights by a lot of awesome people.
Illustrations by Infograpps.com

ISBN: 1508978247 / ISBN-13: 978-1508978244

Contents

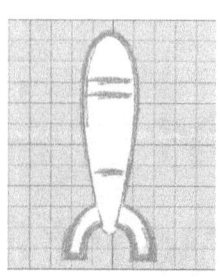

I. Why Social

Understand why this matters.

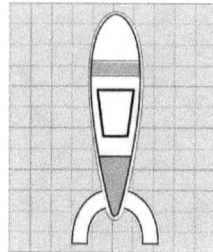

II. Model It

See what's in it for you.

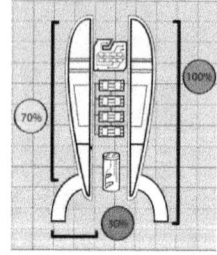

III. Measure It

Make sense and communicate it.

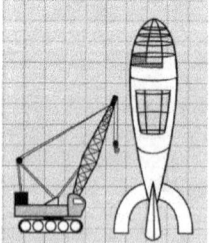

IV. Match It

Integrate it to your life.

I. Why Social

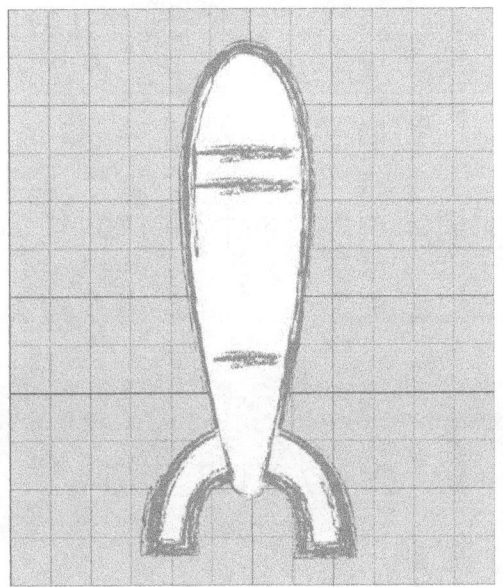

Why managing socially matters.

...

The social dimension is not new, but our attention to it is.

We want to understand it, map it and manage it.

The World is Changing, Again...

The ecosystem in which work gets done is becoming more and more connected. Reaching people, information and goods takes less time (and money). If you don't pay attention to the connections that matter you can quickly become **irrelevant**.

For instance, if you're launching an international campaign and didn't check the brand's phonetic meaning in the local language, you might get an unpleasant surprise. The important connection here is between your brand and its new audience. The words are the same but the message is different.

Mapping the relevant connections doesn't guarantee success, but ignoring them guarantees obsolescence. This book will show you how to identify and monitor the significant links around your work. The next level is where you anticipate them.

> The ability to maneuver through uncertainty is what keeps work in charge of people, instead of computers

The Social Process Model maps your work's relevant connections with: partners, beneficiaries and risks. If you want to discover how irreplaceable your role is for the team, this book is for you! If you want to demonstrate you are the reason why your boss or clients are happy, this book is for you! If you think you can play the risks to your and your client's favor, this book is for you!

At a personal level: How do you monitor the work of co-workers you depend on or outsourcing partners you hired so that you can deliver on time? Or when thinking about your work's contribution, are you aware of how it makes a change throughout the organization? When you describe the impact of work, do you mention how much is attributable to you? If these situations ring a bell it's time to make them part of your way of thinking. This could be perceived as trying to manage the uncertain, and it is! You'll see that what we receive, do and deliver only accounts for about 30% of our work's success. The other 70% is about managing work in its natural form:

SOCIAL

We believe work flows more as a social network and less like an organizational chart (which is good for other purposes, like decision making).

So

MORE

of this.

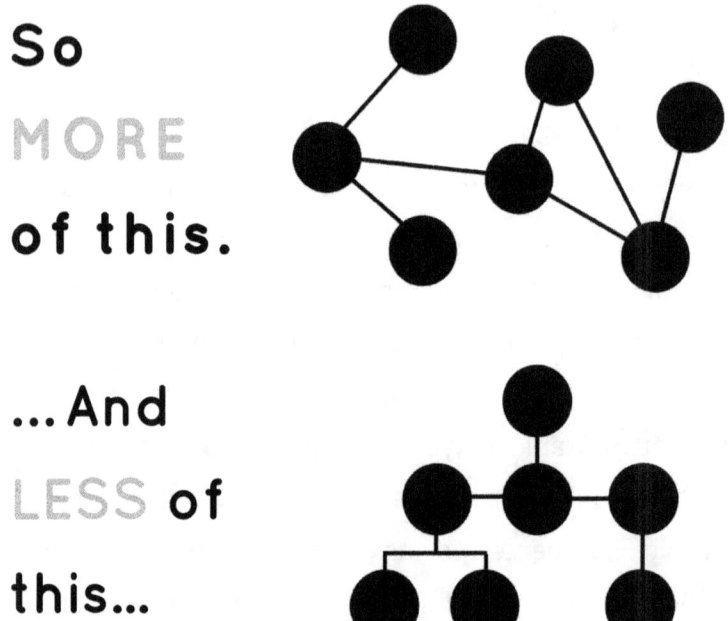

...And

LESS of

this...

The Social Process Model will put you ahead of this change with a simple yet powerful mindset, a guide on using indicators to monitor it and discovering how it matches the systems you already use at work.

Next, you'll see why we came up with the Social Process Model in response to this new work ecosystem, and how it solves the three obstacles to managing work socially.

The 3 Social Concepts

At the end of most planning sessions it's common to see that one BIG PLAN:

But in a work environment with more and more dependability we need to manage in a format that connects at a personal, group and organizational level. We need to see how that BIG Plan connects to the people that will make it happen, those inside and outside of the organization. In that BIG Plan scenario there are three obstacles in managing your work connections:

The beneficiaries changes are given small attention.

That BIG Plan doesn't easily apply at a personal level.

Assumptions are left to fate...

... And you'll manage, right?

Well... If you've been there, done that... don't stop believing. We didn't! And we began testing better ways to manage work and any other social endeavor.

This book's goal is to provide a mindset that answers these questions. Our line of thinking is to build a model that follows naturally how work is being done. This means that **the tool must fit the hand**, and not the other way around.

"Our fix is what follows next."

The development of the Social Process Model began by positively stating that in every planning session we should:

Describe how beneficiaries will be transformed.

Apply the model at the organizational, group and personal level.

Include and track assumptions.

After some thinking, testing and interviewing, we gave a name to each: **impact, process** and **assumptions.** These are the 3 parts of the **Social Process Model.**

IMPACT: Is all about the **change** you make

PROCESS: Is your work **recipe**

ASSUMPTIONS: Uncontrolled **needs**

Example: The Magician

Throughout his performance, a Magician is waiting for the audience to clap like crazy, bring out the Ahhhhs and the Ohhhs!

That is the **IMPACT** or change in the situation that only the Magician can bring. Sometimes, the claps are unexpected, and they're still considered an impact.

Each magician elaborates his unique method of doing things, his "Abracadabra", and keeps it to himself and his team, right or right? It's his **PROCESS** of making magic. In his own words, maybe codified... Because it's his competitive advantage.

Magicians influence the **ASSUMPTIONS** of what is real and what Is not. They build these illusions so you look at what they want you to see. So they don't control what you think or do, but they're aware and act on it. Assumptions are influenced and never controlled.

Now it's time to see the Model and each of the components of the 3 social concepts that make it work.

#workissocial

II. Model It

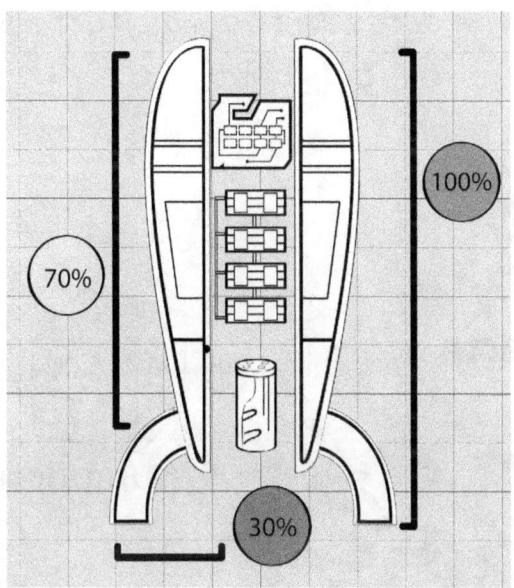

Design your Social Process Model

1. The Social Process model
2. For Example...
3. FAQs

...

The Social Process Model

Manage the ecosystem in which your work gets done

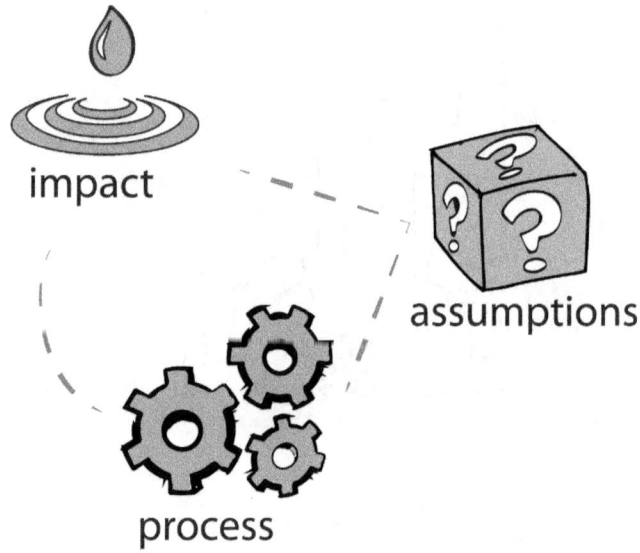

The **Social Process Model** is made for managing work with the three social concepts: impact, process and assumptions.

The Social Process Model

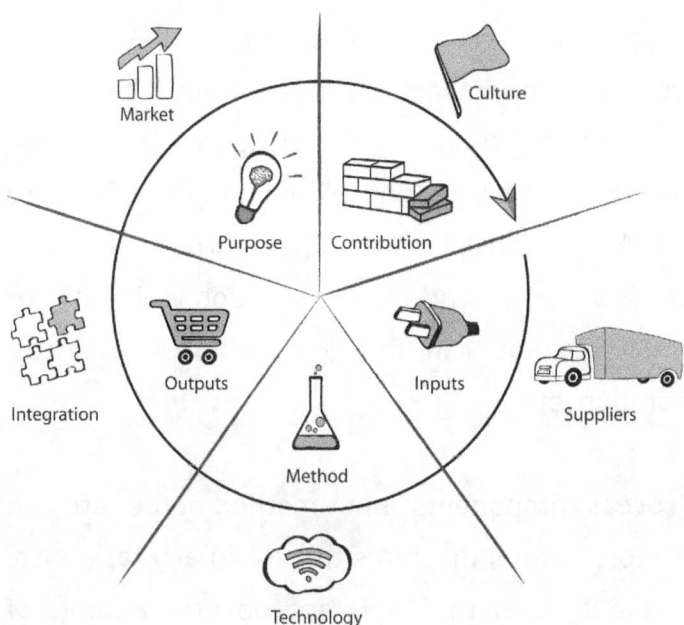

The Model flows clockwise where a process will generate the desired impact, if controlled actions and uncontrolled assumptions become true. The **Process** part of the Model is made of: inputs, method, outputs. The **Impact** is made of purpose and contribution. All five goals or steps have a corresponding **Assumption**, and that makes the ten parts of the Model.

Analyzing the **Impact** in two levels solves our task of *giving beneficiaries adequate attention,* because it requires understanding how we change our beneficiaries situation, and how that change evolves at a bigger scale. In other words, purpose is the direct impact generated, and contribution is the indirect impact. Why is this important? Because you'll be able to demonstrate the change you're responsible for, and how it's a part of a bigger development of which you're not 100% responsible for. The purpose is your hypothesis to prove and the contribution is that bigger goal in which you can find joint-ventures, alliances, collaboration, etc.

The **Process** components: input-method-output are one of the most natural diagrams to explain any task. Also, they make it easier to understand how the outputs of one process become the inputs of other process(es). This solves the challenge of *applying the Model at a personal and group level* with any number of connections.

Finally, the **Assumptions** are the complement to each part of the process and impact. This means they are positive actions we depend on, but are out of our control. We don't decide if they're going to happen or not. We need those assumptions to be true in order to reach our next goal. This seems like risk management, and it is! they're risks stated in a positive way. For every assumption we can choose to influence, complement or any other way of making it happen.

It's more pleasurable and energy efficient for our brains to think of positive things happening, than on avoiding negative things.

To advance one step in the Social Process Model we need the goal and its corresponding assumption to become true. From inputs to impact, there are things we decide on doing and others we influence on happening. This is the nature of work: that in pursuing a goal we're in control of some things, and others we can just influence or avoid.

The model is flexible enough to be explained in multiple ways: from impact to inputs or the other way around. Some will prefer to work first on Impact and process, and then assumptions. Others will want to make sure to finish each component with its corresponding assumption. Like when working: sometimes we start from the end and other times we jump right into the middle of the plan. Any way you want it, the Social Process Model is ready!

#workissocial

For example: **beer!**

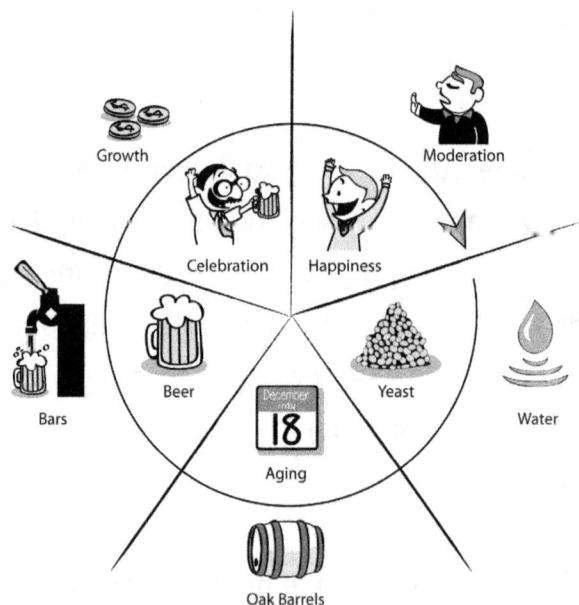

The brewer needs yeast, hops, malted barley and water to start making his beer. There's an assumption that the supplier will deliver these **inputs** on time and with the required quality.

The selected **method** for bringing out the desired flavor is aging. The brewer has his own formula and assumes that the current best technology for him is through oak barrels.

Once the **beer** is ready to ship, the brewer assumes that bars will receive his precious liquid and offer it to the awaited customers.

The **purpose** of this particular beer brand is to help people celebrate, because the brewer said so! And he assumes that there is enough economic prosperity that people can afford having a beer.

Finally, it's useful to know that this particular beer **contributes** to making people happier, and this would help find strategic partners for business. If people drink this beer to celebrate and be happier, the brewer would want them to do so in a moderate way so business can grow.

Now, let us explore each component of the **Social Process Model** in detail to understand what they are and what they are not.

Why are you here, and why now?

*To transform, to make an **impact***

A good impact story tells the <u>positive</u> and <u>negative</u> changes, and also the <u>intentional</u> and <u>unintentional</u> ones. The challenge here is to be aware of the unintentional stuff happening out there that you could leverage. Of course you have to validate your plan's intended goals with one eye, and the other on anything else that is changing. This is the most complete picture you can give about the transformation your beneficiaries are going through.

The goal is to have a complete picture of what's changing, and because impact is systemic we want to monitor it in two levels: **purpose** and **contribution**. The first being the change you and only you cause, the latter an addition to a bigger goal.

Great persuaders leverage on the impact analysis to talk with the emotional brain of their audience. They do this by describing the benefits from the point of view of their beneficiaries. After that, they argue about the strategy and assumptions. The adequate management of impact analysis works brilliantly because our brain is built that way, we first evolved the emotional brain and then the rational one.

The Contribution

Humility is to a person what
contribution is to a process.

The key to identifying a contribution is stating a goal being achieved by two or more independent parties. By independent I mean they don't have the power to manage one another. If a contribution statement is stated as a goal where you're 100% responsible for, then it's not a contribution. In that case you wouldn't be contributing, but generating the whole of it. So the contribution is about seeing yourself as part of a bigger picture.

I've got one question for you, **is *Miss Universe the only contributor to World Peace?***

Ok, so it's clear that world peace is not a one-person job, nor is unemployment, the Team's P&L or negotiating that next deal. In all of these cases there are two or more parties involved. Since we're talking about two or more parties with a bigger common goal, here is where partnerships should be assessed. And what a better way to find a partner than by making sure that greater goal is aligned with your purpose, right or right?

A brewing company could state their bigger goal as "helping people be happier" and identify relevant partners, for example: food manufacturers or local restaurants. This could lead to interesting partnerships, managed at the Contribution level of the Social Process Model.

How aware are we?

Find out how many of your colleagues know your organization's mission statement.

Keeping track of what contributions you're making will help you set the stage for talking about your strategy and performance to audiences outside of your organization. It's the "setting a common ground" part of the speech where you enter the conversation already happening in your audience mind.

The Purpose

What's in it for them?
Yes, for them!

When someone says *"we delivered millions of products"* or *"we have accounted billions of hours of service provided"*, and you feel like there must be something more to that statement, ask them: **What was your product/service hired to do?** And then they'll have to come back with a purpose statement: what their beneficiaries gained. This happens because the default mindset is not putting ourselves in our beneficiaries shoes, and we've got so much in our hands... But worry not! That's why we gave the purpose a part in the Social Process Model. To discover the purpose of your work try comparing your beneficiaries situation:

WITH **AND** WITHOUT **YOU**

That's right! Imagine your beneficiaries **with and without your intervention**... Describe to detail each scenario, include their: emotions, friction points, wins, efforts, resources, and more. What changes between both situations is your purpose, and that is what you make possible for them. When stating your purpose in a simple and powerful sentence, try to distinguish yourself from the competition and any other alternatives. Make an effort to be uncommon and to leave a mark, because it should be as unique as you or your team are. Everyone is trying to maximize customer satisfaction, deliver amazing products and optimize the distribution of content... Your work shouldn't be more of the same! In doing so just don't fall into that dark place where uniqueness loses usefulness.

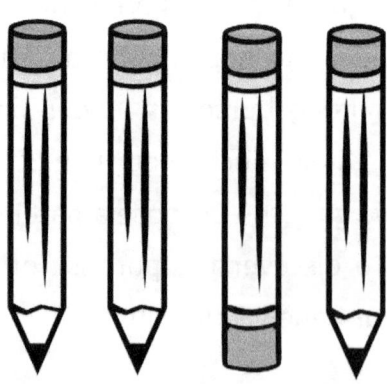

Our recommendation is that you begin the purpose with your BENEFICIARIES, then add a VERB explaining how they change, and finally QUANTIFYING it.

Beneficiaries + Verb + Quantity

By repetition, day by day, the purpose will become your or the organization's mantra. A mindset that reminds you of the change you're after. In the Brewer's example it could be: "Adults in Macklin City celebrate responsibly". That is the difference you're making with your particular Beer and Brand. After you have that clear, go and find out if it's really happening.

The purpose as a mantra will serve as a guide in making better decisions when the Boss can't be consulted.

So far we've been taking the YOU out of the sentence and focusing on THEM (beneficiaries).

#workissocial

The Usual Suspects

If unity is strength, take care of the link, the link!

Inputs, method and outputs are easy to understand: **you receive, you transform and you deliver**. But that's not it, you also have to maintain the link. Your products become inputs to other processes and the other way around.

The process is all about the work you control, and understanding how it connects with other processes.

That job description of yours, with its responsibilities, requirements, skills... Try writing it as a process, in its three sections: outputs, method and inputs. It will make more sense, since that is the way we work. Once you have that done, discover how you link to other processes, like your clients or bosses. What other connections can you make?

The Outputs

Creativity materialized

In your line of work, what would your customers say if you asked them what they want? How would you use that to build the perfect solution? Hardly can beneficiaries articulate the product specifications they need. This part of the Model is for working on that perfect deliverable.

Defining your outputs is about YOU and not about THEM (beneficiaries). Remember that the end user's description is in the Purpose, for example "Young adults celebrate around drinks". Well, if they (beneficiaries) can't get there by themselves, this is where you think of the tools and services you'll provide them to make it happen.

> Start from outputs
> and focus on the
> **opportunity**... **Or** from
> the inputs and focus
> on the **resources**.

One of the most valued skills here is to be creative. To explore alternatives and come up with one that satisfies both ends: you and your beneficiary. Comparing alternatives is one of the best ways to make sure you're choosing the best one. Oh, and alternatives are not re-designs of a solution, but different approaches to solve a problem or seize an opportunity. For instance, a different beer size isn't an alternative, but choosing between a stout or a lager is.

When working on your outputs, the only restriction is to talk about your **deliverables**, that is services or goods that are ready to be used by your beneficiaries. If you get stuck, just prototype. Get a minimum viable product or service and test it. Great thing about prototyping outputs is that you get to iterate more on usable stuff, than when you're thinking about them in presentations and charts.

The Method

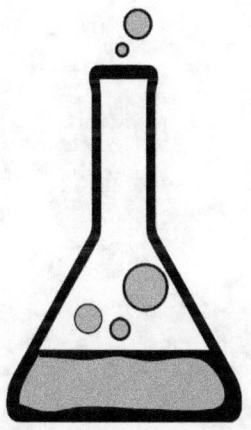

It's the most difficult thing to imitate.

That unique and useful change you want to make in your beneficiaries life, begins here in the method. The choices you make here is what will make your Process different from any other alternatives. Also, the competition you will face depends on how you setup your process, so make sure you're competing on a method you OWN and can do better than anyone else.

Try dressing as a mime, that's easy. Now, try behaving like one. Ok, so you've done it. What about teaching others to follow. See what we mean? And if you want to be great, show them how to be awesome mimes when you're not supervising.

The method needs to be explained with illustrations: lines, circles, boxes, dots and stuff. Somewhat like a treasure map, where you codify the instructions so only your team can understand them. Then it needs to be brought to life through trial and error. Oh! And don't forget the mistakes, something as useful as serendipities can be found in them.

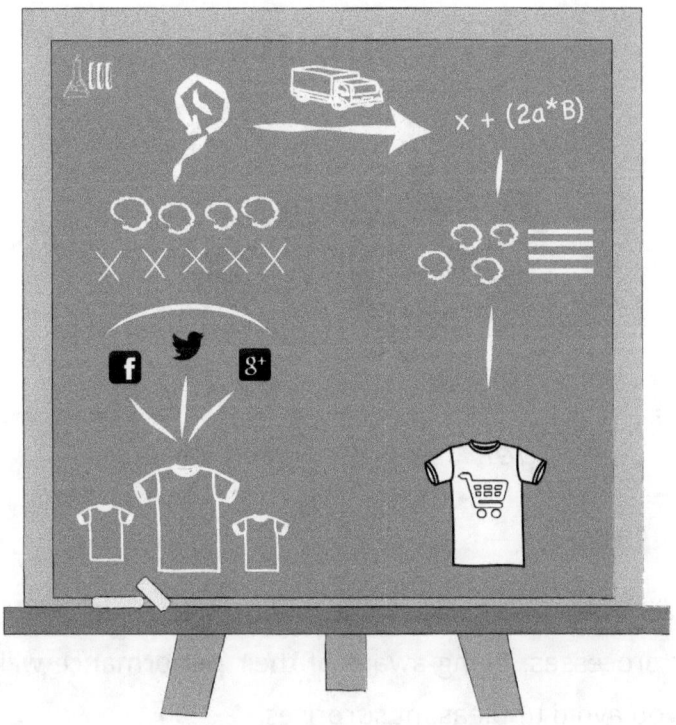

Mapping out a method is not about making people work as robots, it's about leaving a track of the best up-to-date way of doing things and improve on it. Think of it as your backup script for any unexpected event.

The Inputs

Let's get this process started...

The raw material of work will come from the outputs of other processes. Being aware of their performance will help you avoid unpleasant surprises.

About the 3 solutions I explained at the beginning, 2 have been answered so far. The one about:

The model **can be applied** at a personal level, by linking different processes

... Is done by linking one process' outputs as the inputs of another, and vice versa. Your outputs can be the team's or the organization's inputs for your boss to manage, and so on and so forth.
And also the one about:

Describe how beneficiaries will be **transformed**...

... Is solved at the purpose and contribution level of the Social Process Model. Which is aligned to the process outputs in a cause-effect logic.

Now it's time to solve the last part:

Include and track **assumptions**...

Assumptions

Tackling Murphy down!

For every step you take, for every move you make... always be watching your assumptions. Yes, those external things that can change your plan for better or worse without you even noticing until they hit you. As we said, this is an increasingly connected world, so it's imperative that you incorporate assumptions into your way of thinking, your way of managing and your way of communicating.

On the next pitch you hear, ask about the assumptions being considered. For example, ask about the complementary products or services that the product or service is going to work with. What happens if those complements change price, location, quantity? Find out if there is a backup plan.

About assumptions we've said that you can't control them. What you are able to do is: influence, evade, complement, confront them... By considering them into your Social Process Model, you can respond on time before it becomes an unpleasant situation. The actions and reactions will be specific to each of the steps in the Social Process Model. Assumptions at the process level (outputs, method and input) will have to do with your work and assumptions at the impact level (purpose and contribution) will have to do with your beneficiaries.

At the **input** level, what do you depend on? For most, is the punctuality of suppliers. If you assume they will not deliver on time, a preventive action is taken that modifies budgets and time allocation.

At the method level, you assume working with the most convenient **technology**. Upgrades or innovations will change the way you work.

Your outputs will become another's inputs, and you assume **integration** will happen smoothly. Are your deliverables easy to handle by your end users, or do they require something else, out of your control?

At this point of the **Social Process Model** you have delivered your outputs without variations, by managing your assumptions. It's now time to monitor how assumptions will influence the impact you want to generate.

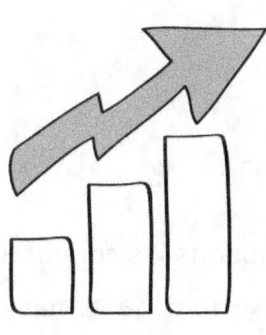

At the purpose level, you assume the **market** conditions like purchasing power or consumer trust are well enough for your beneficiary to trust a change with your intervention.

Want more responsibility and compensation? Handle **assumptions** at a process level. Want more? **Manage** them at the impact level.

At the contribution level, you assume that the solution is being adopted, and revealed in the **culture** or way of life. Then the process becomes sustainable and we can start working on the next challenge.

IMPORTANT Notice

When working on identifying assumptions it's common to come up with a big list, because there are many things that we depend on. The way to filter only those assumptions that matter is to think of their impact and probability.

Very Probable - Not an Assumption

If it has a high probability of happening (more than 50%), don't add it because it will use resources to monitor that could be better spent on other tasks.

Probable - Yes, it's an Assumption

If you aren't certain that an assumption will happen (30% - 70%), include it to monitor its progress over time.

Not Probable - Bad, very very bad...

If the probability of happening is very low, you're in trouble, since you depend on this for achieving your goals. Modify your plan so that you depend on a more probable assumption.

If you're documenting and learning about your work's assumptions, in time they'll change from highly unexpected and uncontrollable situations to expected and manageable. We encourage you and your organization to master the art of managing assumptions and always be on the look for new challenges.

This implies testing and documenting your strategy to learn the useful and un-learn the not useful, a task that can be better done with indicators (more in following chapter). Assumption management will always be a profitable road to differentiate yourself, your team and your company.

#workissocial

For Example...

The Model in action

This is how the Social Process looks applied to three different scenarios: a private company, a public office and an NGO.

The three examples represent our view of what needs to be managed. Different Social Process Models can show other views of what needs to be managed

Get a copy of the
worksheet at
socialprocessmodel.com

Remember that:

- **Purpose** goals talk about your beneficiary, not about you nor your product.
- **Assumptions** are out-of-your-control situations that need to happen in order to advance to the next step in the model.

Private Company – Cleaning

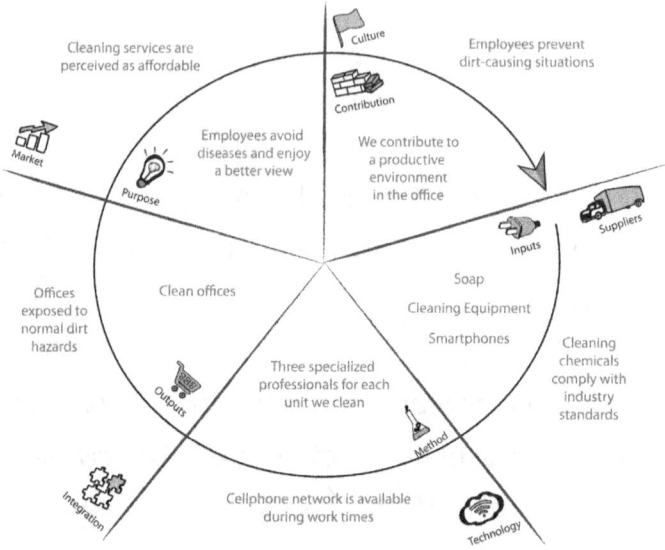

Public Office – Parks

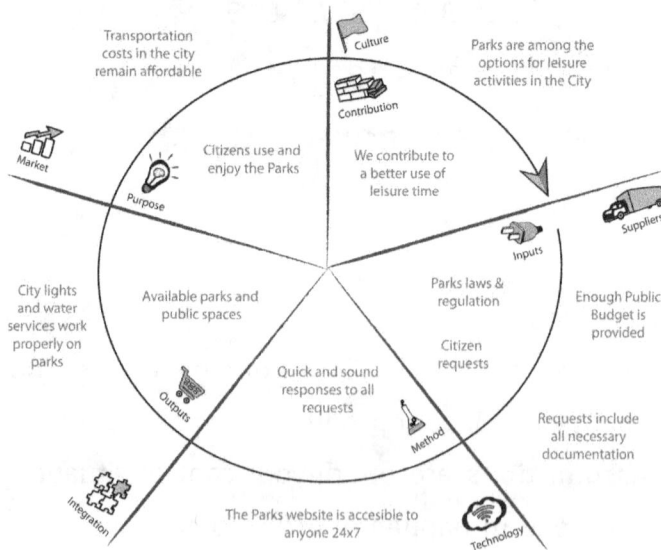

NGO – Housing

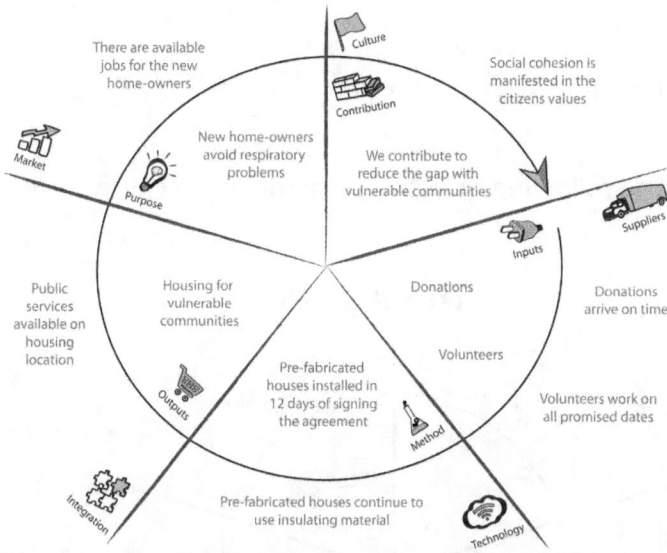

Done with examples! Already done yours? Did you hack the Model already? Share it!

#workissocial

The FAQs

Just in case you haven't figured it out yet

The following questions are meant to clarify.

The Inputs

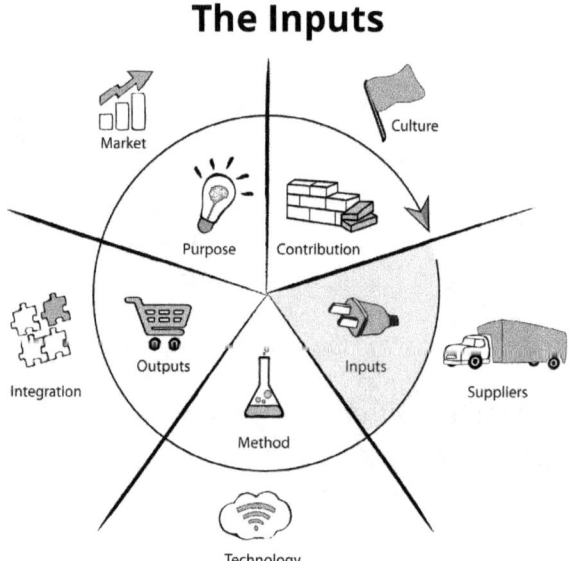

What do you need to begin work? What do you buy for work?

Are materials, services and intangibles part of your inputs?

Inputs are all things which if NOT available, work can't begin. What's on your checklist?

The Suppliers

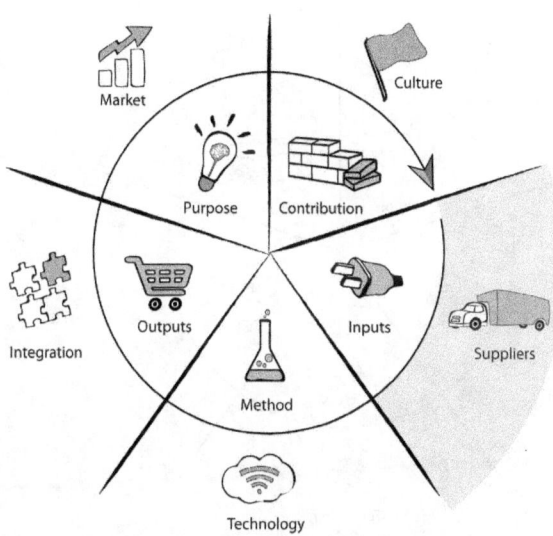

What's the most important thing that you depend on and your supplier controls?

Historically, what are the most common delays with suppliers?

Are there any quality assurance audits needed before delivery?

The Method

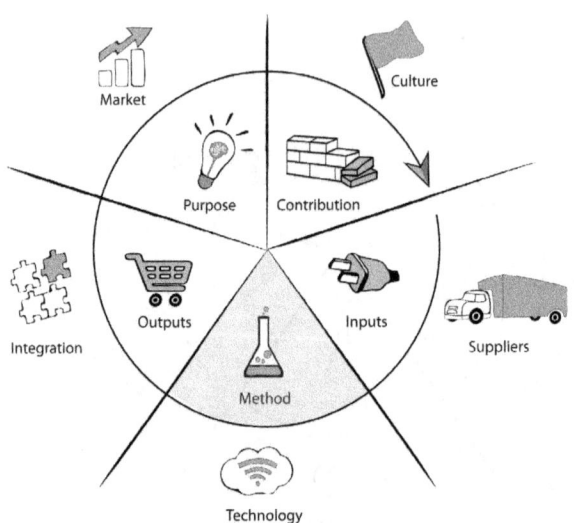

What tasks are on you calendar?

What's your recipe? Your way of working?

If you write about how to replicate your work, what would it say?

What differentiates your work from other engineers, lawyers, designers?

The Technology

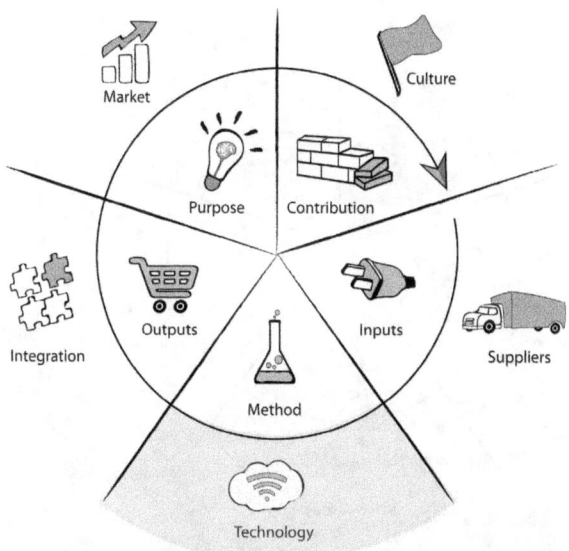

How will a change in the current version of your software/hardware modify your method?

Is there a common language, rules or standards in your line of work?

Will there be wifi when we get there?

The Outputs

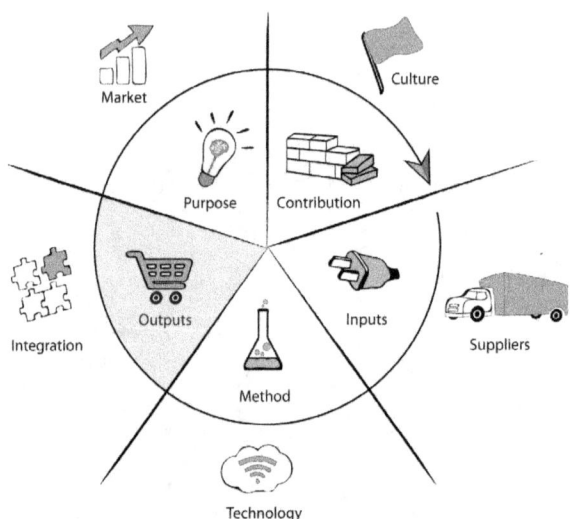

What are you delivering to your customer?

When your work is done, how do you describe what you have produced?

How is your product or service different from the competition?

What does the specifications sheet say?

The Integration

Is your product/service being used as a part of a bigger one?

Does your product need inputs of any sort? Energy, gas or else?

What are the complementary products/services that your outputs depend on to work at their best?

The Purpose

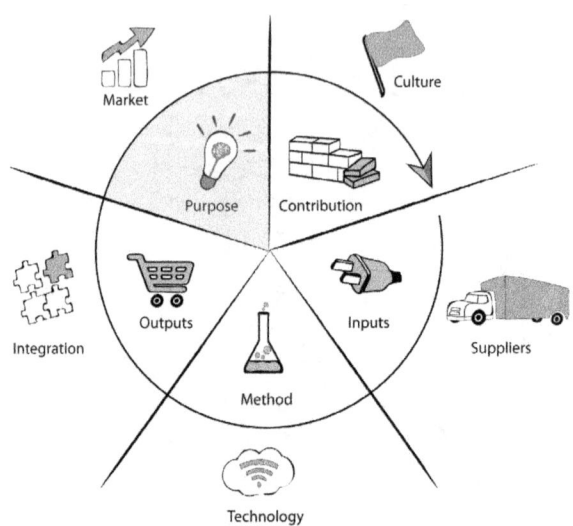

What is your product/service hired to do?

How will your customer be better with your work than without it?

The purpose is not about you! It's about your customers! What about them?

What would happen (not to you) if you didn't work? The opposite scenario is the purpose.

The Market

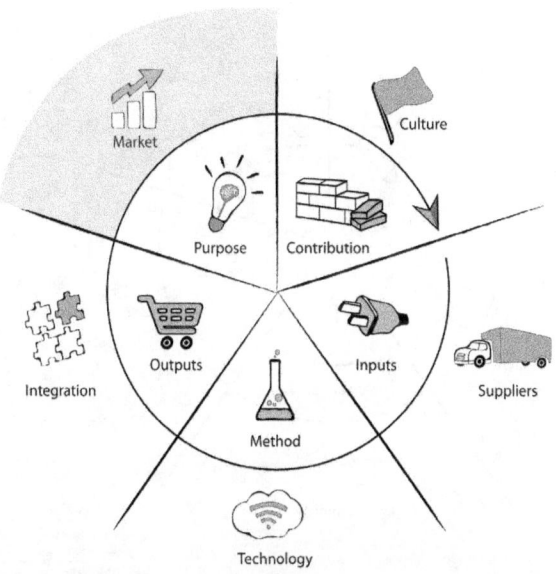

What needs to be solved, so that your consumer achieves the purpose at the fullest?

Is there anything that is out of your consumer's control (and yours) that can impede them from changing for the better?

The Contribution

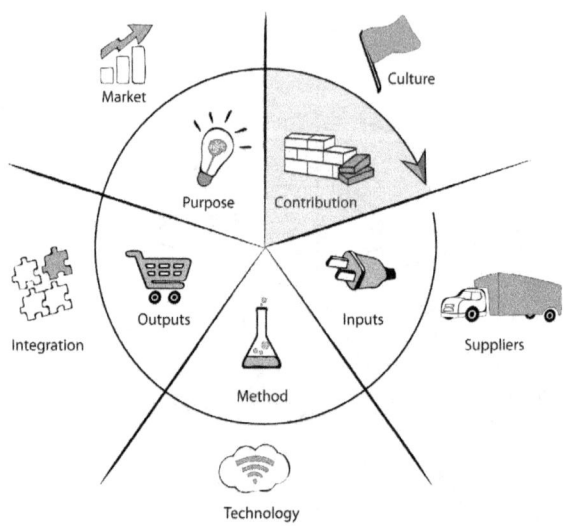

What bigger goal are you part of? Bigger than your purpose!

If the goal is 100% your responsibility, then it's the purpose. If it's less than 100% it's your contribution, right or right?

Are you partnering with someone else (from another organization)? Then you're both contributing to a bigger goal.

The Culture

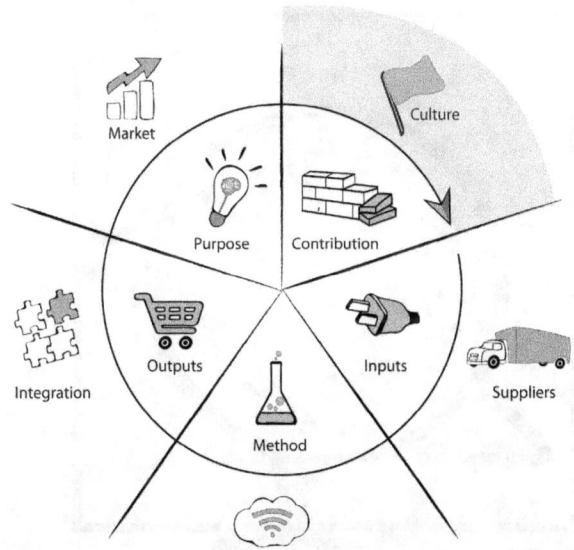

How can that Big Goal, which you're contributing to, be a part of the culture?

What needs to happen (outside your control) so that you don't worry about the same problem again and again?

Mastering Change, Again...

The world is changing, and you're shaping the change. You own your work connections and have identified that which makes you irreplaceable. On top of that you're focused on your client's change and making sure its for the better. And above all, assumptions are being played to your favor and that of your clients. The Social Process Model is the productivity app for your brain that will take your management skills to the next level of change: social. It will empower you to:

- Manage relevant **connections** and remain valuable.
- Describe **change** that you generate.

- Include **assumptions** and anticipate them.
- Use a common **language** for connecting your work to colleagues and external parties.

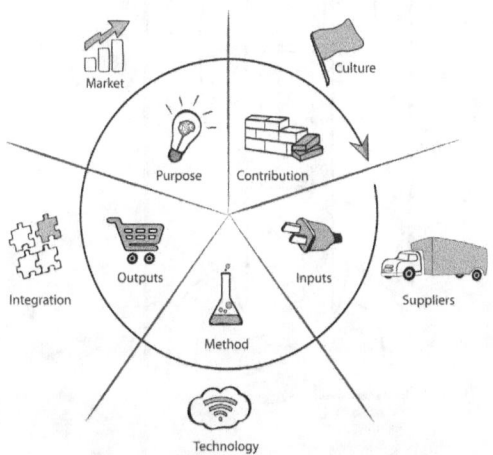

On the next parts you'll find content about indicators matching the Model with other work systems. On the indicators part you will learn how to measure the progress of your Social Process Model, with simple and clear indicators! No fancy talk. On the last part you'll go into how to match the Social Process Model with other tools that you might already use.

Go for it!

#workissocial

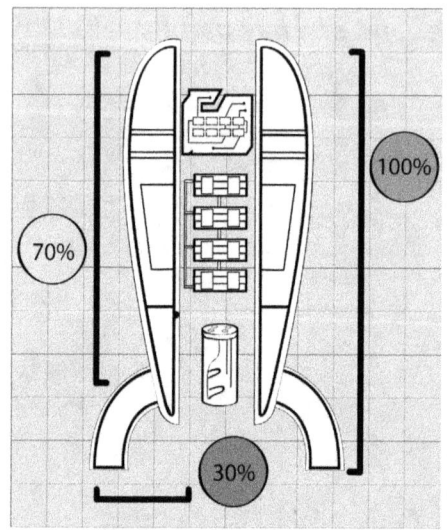

III. Measure It

Monitor your Social Process Model

1. Measure to Manage
2. BS-Free Measuring
3. Measure the Measure

...

Measure to Manage

"Indicators are simple", repeat after me...

How do you differentiate success
from failure?

How do you assure you're
rewarding success and not
failure?

How can others learn from your
success?

If you think that anticipating in the right moment and with the right intensity is good for business, the following lines are for you. Indicators are all about gathering information that matters, and acting on it. We'll make it simple, easy and straightforward. From now on you'll learn how to measure the Social Process Model's **Evolution**.

First things first. Because the indicators' values change over time, we need to re-arrange the flow of the Social Process Model into a monitoring friendly display. That is from circle to columns, so we can show indicator updates to the right, or in other words the evolution of an indicator. The assumptions will be monitored on each indicator's update because their probability of happening also changes over time. Wrapping it up, when you update an indicator you also update the assumption's probability of happening.

Next we'll show how we go from the model view (left) to the monitoring view (right)

The Social Process Model

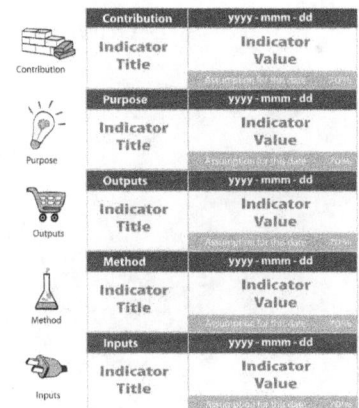

Contribution	yyyy - mmm - dd
Indicator Title	Indicator Value
Assumption for this date 70%	
Purpose	yyyy - mmm - dd
Indicator Title	Indicator Value
Assumption for this date 70%	
Outputs	yyyy - mmm - dd
Indicator Title	Indicator Value
Assumption for this date 70%	
Method	yyyy - mmm - dd
Indicator Title	Indicator Value
Assumption for this date 70%	
Inputs	yyyy - mmm - dd
Indicator Title	Indicator Value
Assumption for this date 70%	

1- Begin with The Social Process Model

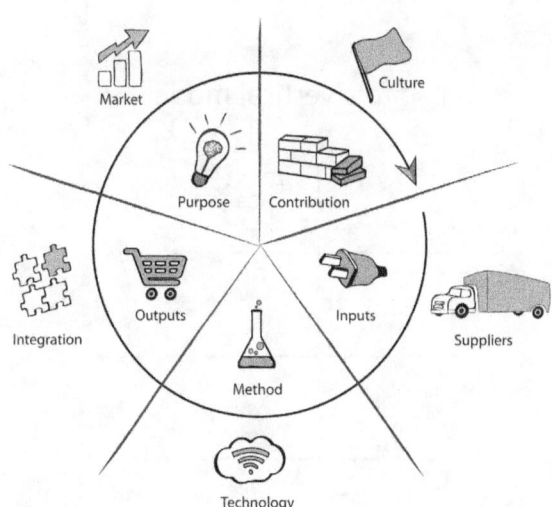

2- Unwrap the model...

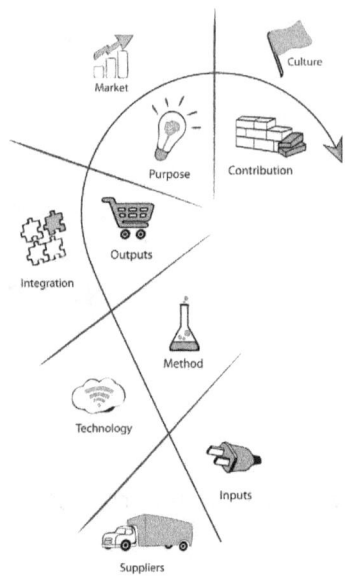

3- ... Into a vertical model

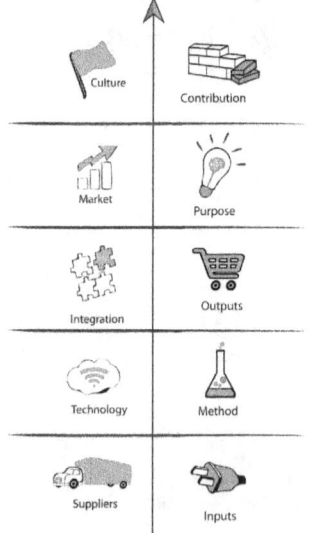

4- Now indicator titles or names go on the left column. Indicator values and assumptions go in the right column.

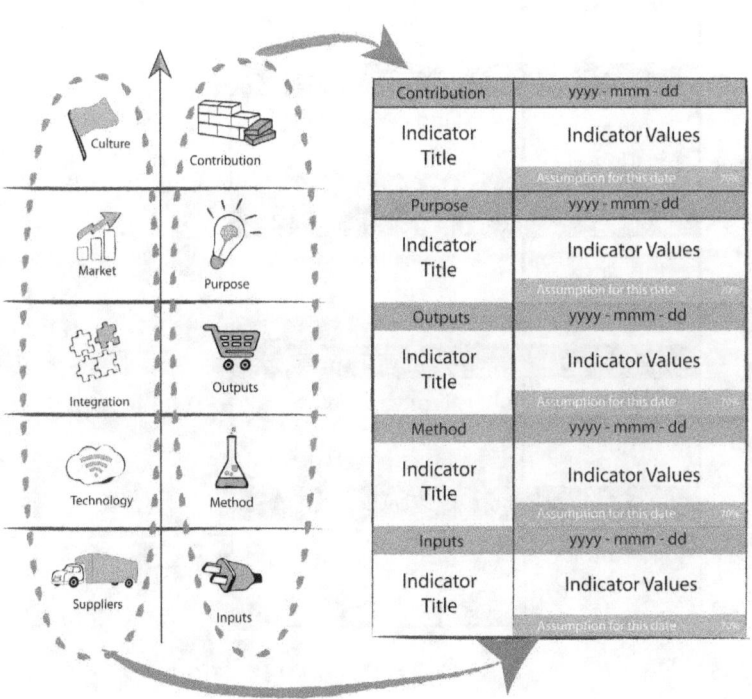

5- For each update to an indicator you'll add a column with the new value and their assumption.

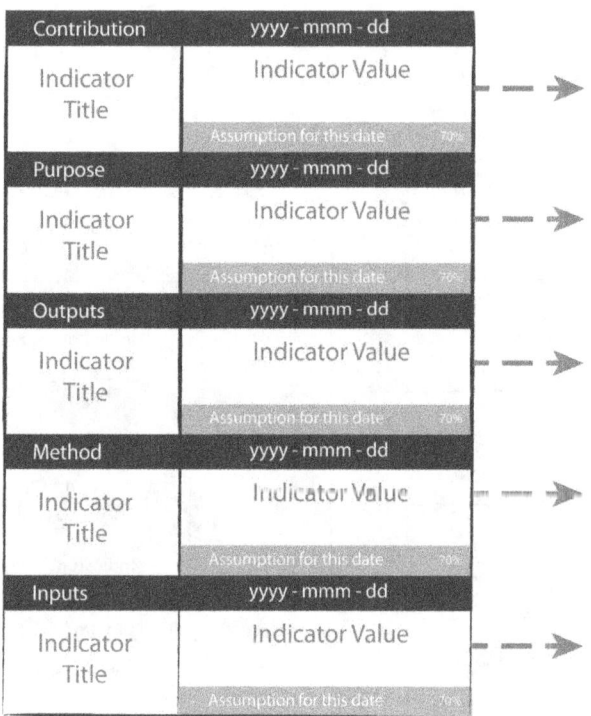

Now you have a monitoring-friendly view of the Model that can show change over time. This will be useful when generating reports from one monitoring database to different stakeholders.

How many pages do your (teams, company…) reports have? Can you make a One Page Report with enough information to make a statement?

If you could use the Social Process Model as the format for a one page report, how many time-frames would you include as columns? Is portrait view better than landscape?

Share your awesomeness at #workissocial.

Monitoring **Indicators**

To track an indicator all you need is: **physical** and **financial** values, in their **planned** and **actual** scenarios.

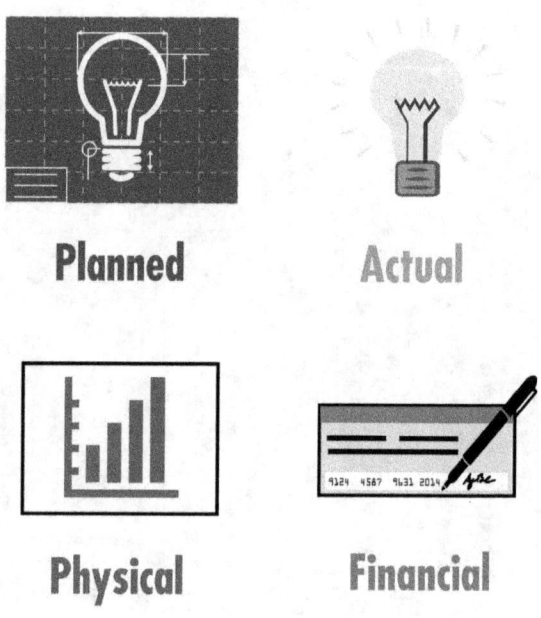

Planned   **Actual**

Physical   **Financial**

Of course you can add more variables, we're starting with the minimum viable ones that you probably already use. Now that you know what to monitor, arrange them in a table view.

	Planned	Actual
Physical	10,500	11,000
Financial	$3,800	$3,500

With this 2 by 2 table you can make all the basic calculations to monitor an indicator. It also works for other classification systems like: results and operative indicators or lagging and leading indicators.

For every update, add: planned, actual, physical and financial data. This will allow you to run multiple analysis with the same database of information.

Adding these four variables will make the table look a bit more complicated, but remember that with great data comes great analysis.

	Contribution		Planned	Actual
Contribution	Indicator Title	P	Physical	Physical
		$	Financial	Financial
	Assumption for this date			70%
Purpose	Purpose		Planned	Actual
	Indicator Title	P	Physical	Physical
		$	Financial	Financial
	Assumption for this date			70%
Outputs	Outputs		Planned	Actual
	Indicator Title	P	Physical	Physical
		$	Financial	Financial
	Assumption for this date			70%
Method	Method		Planned	Actual
	Indicator Title	P	Physical	Physical
		$	Financial	Financial
	Assumption for this date			70%
Inputs	Inputs		Planned	Actual
	Indicator Title	P	Physical	Physical
		$	Financial	Financial
	Assumption for this date			70%

Now *let's get interesting*

Frequency, assumptions and the indicator's profile.

Frequency

Tony is a well known DJ who keeps the crowd up all night. One of his KPIs is the amount of people on the dance floor.

How often should He monitor this?

As often as change can happen

At every level of your Social Process Model you can decide how often change must be understood.

10-May-2015, 10:30 am

	Planned	Actual
Physical	10,500	11,000
Financial	$3,800	$3,500

When the frequency of your indicators doesn't match that of your business, unnecessary stuff gets piled up.

Are you timing it adequately?

Assumptions

Now that we know how to set the formula and frequency of the indicators, let's work on assumptions. As said before, for every update on an indicator, you'll also update the corresponding assumption, and its probability of happening. This means assumptions can change during the lifetime of the indicator.

Remember: Assumptions are uncontrolled and expected situations, that change over time

You don't control assumptions, and you need them to happen in order to meet your goal. An assumption will always be something under the control of someone external to the owner of the process.

For example, when you check the weather you're making sure it's appropriate for your plans. *Am I right or am I right?* In the DJ example, an important assumption could be that the electricity is up and running for his equipment to work properly. If there were a chance of this not happening, the DJ would need to keep an eye on it and have a backup plan.

In the indicator's table the assumption is displayed at the bottom. It's important to monitor assumptions with their probability of happening. In this example, we are assuming there is a 70% probability that the electricity will work well, and that other 30% could mean, for example, that in the past there have been a few times when the electricity outlet can't handle the speakers.

10-May-2015, 10:30 am

	Planned	Actual
Physical	10,500	11,000
Financial	$3,800	$3,500

Assumption: electricity working properly during the party (70%)

So, when an assumption has a high probability of happening it should be good news, because your success depends on it.

When the probability is low you should be prepared with a plan that is: contingent, corrective or preventive. The cost of making the assumption happen will most definitely influence your indicator's financial values.

Indicator's **Profile**

For every indicator you will write once, CETERIS PARIBUS, its profile. That way you don't have to go explaining all of it, but instead have them read the following information:

Definition
A clear, precise way of describing what you are measuring and what you are not measuring.

Formula
How do you come up with your result? Do you add, multiply, use an index, interview people, follow a lead?

Physical unit of measure
Define what you are measuring: minutes, clients, orders, tons, etc.

Financial unit of measure
How do you value the unit you are measuring: dollars, pesos, euros, etc.

Deadline
When will you reach your goal?

Frequency

How often will you monitor progress towards the goal?

Responsible for planning

Who submits the planned values: physical and financial.

Responsible for updating

Who submits the actual values: physical and financial. It could be the same person responsible for planning.

Signaling ranges

For a quick view at the indicator's performance you can use color codes. This will be most helpful when looking at multiple indicators in the same report.

Green - **Good**

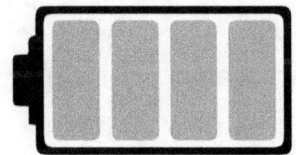

Current progress is as expected. There is no need for correction.

Yellow - **It's a warning**

Performance is not as expected, it can go good or bad. Needs attention.

Red - Bad, go fix it

Definitely <u>bad</u> and in need of urgent correction. If it continues, goals won't be met.

Orange - Outlier

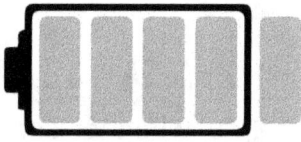

Current status is <u>too good to be true.</u> Review the evidence and the formula.

Imagine your battery displayed with a 125% of charge!

We're done with indicator stuff, and ready to master their quality and communicate them with a common language.

#workissocial

BS-Free Sources

"Thou shalt not use poor data to measure"

Remember when you responded what was most convenient to you, even if it wasn't the most adequate answer? Because you don't want THAT happening with the data being used for your indicators, we'll go over some ideas on how to prevent getting poor data.

Next time you're doing research, will you ask or observe?

What's wrong?

Nothing

What makes the difference between indicators is the quality of the source.

Most of the metrics and formulas on best practices can be found online. The competitive advantage lies in the quality of the source.

This is what you need to know about designing your sources of data:

- Where: **Scope and Depth**
- To be or not to be **NOTICED**
- **How much** i$ much

Combine between scope and depth

The poll is a great example of going large on scope, and that provides a general idea of things. The interview (either direct or indirect), in contrast, delivers a more deep understanding of a very small sample, usually smaller than the poll one.

Which way to go? Or both? The great thing about polls is they provide a quick picture of a current situation.

What's great about interviews is a detailed study into how a subject behaves under specific circumstances.

Your decision will be somewhere in between:

Situation A: Not Sure: If you're not clear about what you're looking for, start with an in-depth research. This means observing at a high level of detail, how a situation evolves without you intervening. Then you'll understand how a situation emerges and evolve.

Situation B: I'm sure: If you think you are sure of what your questions are and what you need to find out, go ahead with a poll and figure out **where** the action is.

To be or not to be notised

Aha! That's the question when designing your approach to gather data. You see, if I ask you: **How much would you pay for a tele-transportation system from work to home?** you'd probably go down and approach this as a negotiation.

What if I observe how people decide on traffic situations, for example how much they pay on a toll highway over the next best alternative. Those are revealed preferences, whereas the previous example are declared preferences.

There is a quote about Henry Ford that goes something like this "If I had asked people what they wanted...

... they would've **told** me: a bigger horse"

How Much I$ Much?

You know it's going to cost time and money. Best you can do is match the budget to the interest of acquiring data. You can be in any of these situations:

Original

The highest cost and most accurate source comes from generating new information, specific to the goal being achieved. Consider every step from planning to executing.

Used

Using the results of a published research is less costly than generating it, and not so accurate since the data was obtained for other purposes.

Role play

The lowest cost of acquiring information is making assumptions about what can happen, like doing role play. In this scenario we suggest you validate these assumptions with as many iterations as possible as you go forward with your work.

Done with the sources! Remember they mark the difference between bad and awesome indicators. Next section is all about how to *talk indicators!*

#workissocial

Measure the Measure

Never again be deceived by complex indicator speeches

It's common to hear or say that a process is efficient or sustainable, but are you sure you and your audience have the same meaning of the words your are saying? Really? Go ask someone how they define the following words and then compare them to your definition.

Impact: The positive and negative, intentional and unintentional effects of any intervention.

Sustainable: The degree to which your solution is being adopted by your beneficiaries.

Relevant: The degree to which the goals satisfy the needs of your beneficiaries.

Efficient: The relation between the outputs and inputs of any action.

Effective: The degree to which the goals are being met.

When talking about indicators we often say these words as if they would find their place somewhere in the sentence, or maybe because they sound right, and it gets confusing when we make further analysis. Our next step is to illustrate what each of these dimensions measure and clear this confusion once and for all.

The Measures Diagram

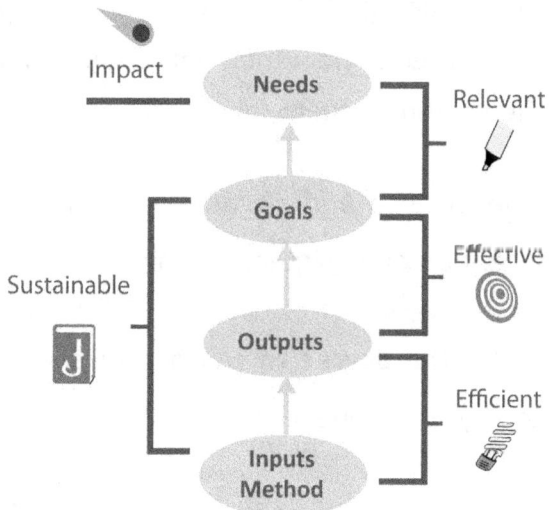

Many terms used for describing performance can be classified with this diagram. For instance quality, understood as the extent to which something meets a standard, is a measure of effectiveness. Profitability is a measure of efficiency, as it compares cost with revenue.

Impact

The positive and negative: intentional and unintentional effects of any intervention.

Most only care about the intentional and positive effects, and that's not a bad thing! It's just incomplete. Noticing the whole picture implies to be as objective as possible, meaning that more than two sources come up with the same conclusion. Remember! Un-intentional and negative also count.

The key to measuring the impact is to see how the needs changed after the intervention. Document your beneficiaries situation before and after your work. Use pictures, diagrams, notes, interviews and what suits them best.

Relevance

The degree to which the goals satisfy the needs of your beneficiaries.

If you read the same text a couple of months later it's possible that you will highlight different words. Because they're relevant to your circumstances. By relevant we mean that which substitutes the current state of things. If you're applying the Social Process Model to your life it means that it's being relevant to you.

If you want to be relevant you've got to manage the tension between their (beneficiaries) needs and what you can set as goals. That tension arises from what you can promise based on restrictions and what beneficiaries need based on their ideas.

Effectiveness

The degree to which the goals are being met.

This one is the simplest of them all, no wonder it's the most used. What matters is reaching the goal. This measuring dimension doesn't consider the resources needed to achieve the goals.

Quality is a form of measuring effectiveness, meaning if something or someone performs according to a set of standards.

Efficiency

The relation between the outputs and inputs of any work being done.

Because resources are limited we want to be sure we get the most out of them, and that's what we think when explaining efficiency. It compares what goes out with what came in.

When measuring efficiency we don't know if the best alternative was chosen, that has to do with being relevant and making an impact. With efficiency we discover doing: more with less, more with the same or same with less.

Sustainable

The degree to which your solution is being adopted by your beneficiaries.

A solution has to be sustained by someone, carried on by a person or group. Speaking WORK this means it's being sustained by you or your beneficiaries. You could do this forever, meaning sustaining the solution, and that's not bad. The thing is that when you compete, you need to innovate and for that you need space. If your beneficiaries adopt the solution as their way of life, you can occupy your time in the next challenge. Teach them to fish!

When your beneficiaries start to solve the problem by themselves you can move to solve a new situation, improve life at a higher level. If you don't... your competition probably will.

#workissocial

Balancing your Dimensions

Now that you know the concepts you can apply them with confidence. There is no good or wrong combination, there is only great alignment between the dimensions your indicators measure and your business model intentions.

A manufacturer in a competitive market should use good efficiency indicators to benchmark his work processes. If this doesn't matter then he should be a very good artist or craftsman focusing on relevance and impact. Innovation-focused organizations would emphasize on sustainability indicators, so they can know when a user can adopt a new product or service, and of course that should be relevant.

Done with indicators! Follow to the next chapter and you'll see how the Social Process Model can be matched to your day-to-day tools.

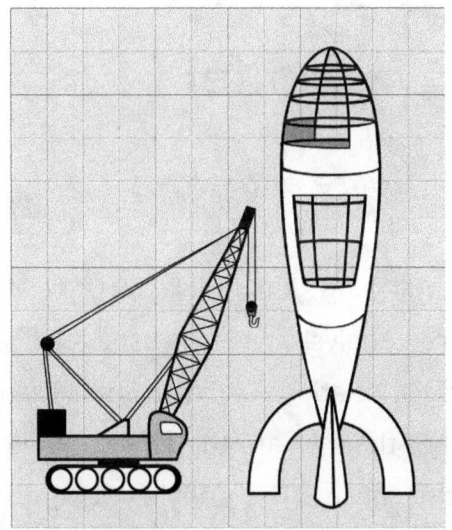

IV. Match It

Match your Social Process Model

1. To Causes & Effects
2. To People and HR
3. To Budgets

...

Build your Social Process Model

Cause and effect...

The tool that will help you build your Social Process Model is the Tree Analysis, which is used for discovering cause and effect relations to a given situation. The branches (top) of the tree are the effects, and the roots (bottom) are the causes. The unifying statement at the middle is the situation at hand.

The purpose of this tool is to help in identifying the cause-effect relationships where we can work on, so that we change the situation for the best.

Clarifying the Situation

We'll begin from where you're standing, that's the situation. If you describe the situation as the absence of a solution, you'll never know if you're working with the best alternative. This happens when you define the situation starting with "I need", because that implies a solution. What we're saying is that if you can spare some time to deepen your understanding of the situation you'll come up with a better diagnosis.

How would you better describe a problem/opportunity?

Do you need a car? Or do you need affordable transportation?

#workissocial

Clarifying Causes and Effects

After coming up with a situation statement you can add, in a tree shaped upward, its effects or consequences. *If this problem/opportunity takes place or continues, it would provoke: effect 1, effect 2, etc.*

Now do the same with the causes, but put them downwards. *What is causing this problem/opportunity to take place is: cause 1, cause 2, etc.*

A complete tree analysis provides a snapshot of the current situation, broken into actionable pieces of information.

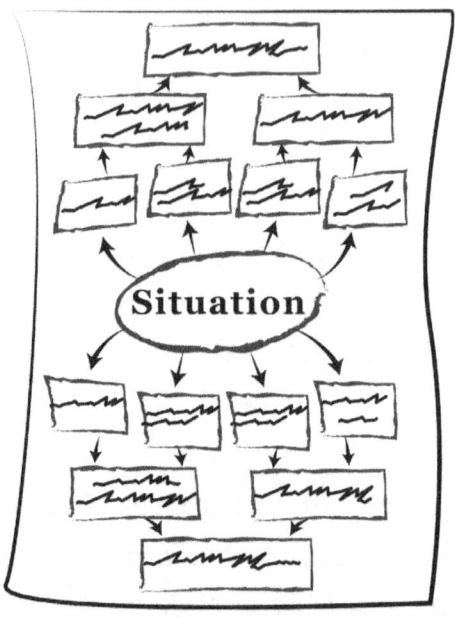

The effects and causes can have two or more levels, depending on how much detail you're putting into the analysis. Add as much levels in the effects section as needed to achieve a **global common effect**, that is a result of all previous effects. With causes, the last level should be a close and actionable cause. That is something that can be scheduled or managed.

Now, transfer the Tree Analysis to the Social Process Model. The common global effect becomes the contribution. The situation in the tree analysis becomes the purpose of the process. The causes you want to work on become your method, the ones which you want to acquire become your inputs, and the ones others will do become your assumptions.

You can come back to the Tree Analysis if you need to redesign your Social Process Model or even if you want to present it in a more visual way. It's still the best tool for synthesizing day-to-day information into a process.

Match the Social Process Model to PEOPLE

Taking the Job Description to a whole new level

The Job Description contains what you've agreed to work on. It's a statement of your value to a team or organization and of the expectations looking forward. But, it can't quite serve the purpose of managing the daily interactions of the job. It's not like you've attached to it several progress reports or updated it with every new assignment, and we want to take it to the next level! That is, after you're hired.

People will always be the most valuable resource of any organization. People are the most flexible asset of them all. We can adapt to any situation, and yet our management systems have to keep up with us. Including our job description.

Do you remember your job description? Have you updated it? Have some fun and ask the same to your colleagues.

How would you update your work description? And how often?

The match between the Job Description and the Social Process Model will help you manage your professional career on a daily basis and with a social way of thinking. You'll be capable of anticipating on assumptions, understanding the impact of your work and keeping track of the responsibilities you've assumed.

We'll do that by migrating the components in a Job description: responsibilities, justification, and requirements into the Social Process Model and adding what's needed. To explain the match we'll follow a bottom-top direction: that is beginning with the inputs.

Inputs - **what you get**

The part of the Job Description that talks about the Organization assets and all that you'll have at your disposal in order to begin work will be the inputs of your Social Process Model. Examples are: data, applications, subordinates, team members, etc. It's everything you'll receive from either inside the company or outside from suppliers.

Method - **what you bring**

The section of the Job Description you usually have the most interest in, will become the Social Process Model's

Method, and that is: the requirements. It's the reason you've been hired. The skills and knowledge you bring to the team. It includes all the certifications, experience, knowledge... that are needed to get the job done. In time, the method is updated by the innovations you incorporate into your way of working.

Outputs - what you deliver

Whatever deliverables the Job Description mentions will become your Social Process Model Outputs. All items mentioning a deadline will be displayed here. This are the products and services you deliver into other Processes.

Purpose - your clients/boss

This is the reason why your job is needed in the organization. So if the Job Description mentions why your position became a need, that will sure make up for the purpose. Another purpose statement in the Job Description could be the notes on how you'll be evaluated. Any mentions of your beneficiaries situation and how you can make it better sure is a purpose statement, but it has to be a direct relationship, immediate to your actions otherwise it's a contribution statement.

Contribution - **how you add up**

Comment on how you work is part of a bigger enterprise are the words contribution statements are made of. Any mentions of words like partnerships or associations are probably related to contributions. Identifying your next career goal is a way of knowing how your contribution should look like. Understanding contributions will also help you notice potential partners that are sharing the same higher common goal either inside or outside the organization.

Now you've seen the match between the Social Process Model and the job description. Your job's management system is now a tool for managing your work goals. The purpose of matching this two systems is for you to make the most out of your time, by uncovering the relations of your job with beneficiaries, colleagues and external parties.

Use a system to update,
plan and manage your job
(description) socially, and
you'll find amazing
opportunities for synergy.

People management can be more easily done if thinking in terms of social processes interacting with each other. This doesn't mean we encourage you to treat people like objects, but to organize work around: contributions, purpose, outcome, methods and inputs.

We have used the Job Description here as the example of how to match the Social Process Model way of thinking into people or relations management. There are other possibilities to be explored.

Where will you go from
here?

#workissocial

Match the $ocial Proce$$ Model to BUDGET$

Access budgets with a zoom

Budgets have a match with the financial values of your indicators. The financial values include two of the four basic values in the indicator's matrix: planned-actual and financial-physical. You can either see a budget broken down into accounts or into indicators, which is what I propose here. Both views serve a purpose: order and management.

> What purpose do the budgets in your organization serve?

In the Social Process Model view of budgets, the sum of individual budgets will build a group budget, and the sum of all the groups or individual budgets will make the organization's budget. Very clear, it's about dividing budgets into actionable indicators.

For tracking the planned and actual incomes and expenses, that are related to indicators in your Social Process Model, we go to the Indicator 2 by 2 table, specifically to the financial values boxes.

10-May-2015, 10:30 am

	Planned	Actual
Physical	10,500	11,000
Financial	$3,800	$3,500

Assumption: electricity working properly during the party (70%)

In a financial or accounting way of thinking you would divide a budget into accounts related to the flow of money. In the Social Process Model you can arrange the same budget into accounts related to actions (process) and results (impact). We think this is a better way to monitor budget decision within individuals, teams and organizations because instead of looking at accounts you'll be seeing a budget in the form of a process.

Money is an information system about supply and demand options. As you have access to more options, you'll decide more efficiently.

Simple enough! After setting up your goals for every level of your Social Process Model, you'll allocate the budget into the planned financial value of your indicators. This is a time for making trade-offs with the budget you have, or with finding ways to get more resources to reach your goals.

In deciding how much money will be needed to complete a task, you will also consider the effect that assumptions can have on your goals. For example, if the assumption you depend on has a low probability of happening you might include some extra budget for the efforts on making it happen. The end result here is managing your budget socially, in relation to activities, results and assumptions. This is a way of using money as means to an end.

#workissocial

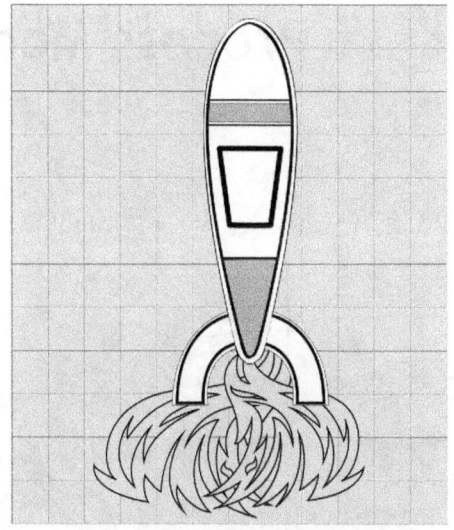

IV. Move It

Monitor your Social Process Model

4. This is It
5. About the Author

...

This is it!

The Social Process Model

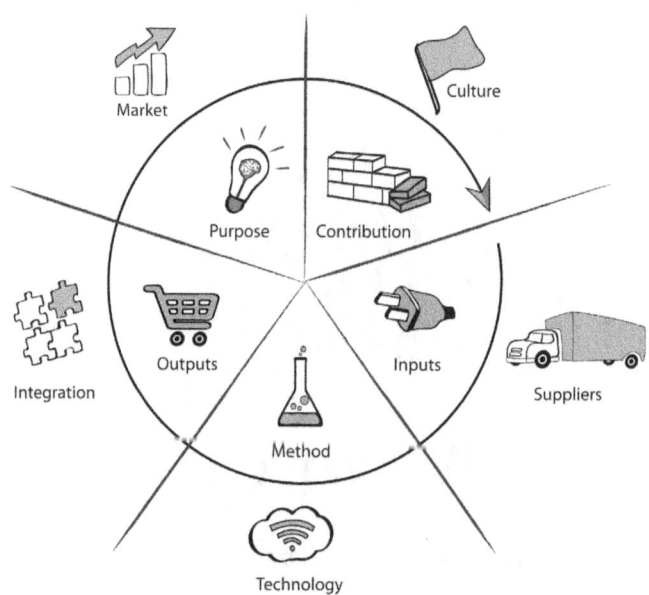

As with every upgrade, you're going to need space for the Social Process Model to become a part of your and your team's way of thinking. In doing so we're aware that you will deal with emotions of all sorts, the relevant question is: are you aware? Yes! We believe awareness is the key to making this change happen.

In the transition from a conscious way of thinking to unconscious mastery of the Social Process Model do notice the opportunities to "make room" for the Model to be tested, tuned and internalized to your way of working. If you hear someone talking about the customers change, try to identify the relationship that it has to outputs and contributions and make sense of how that matters to you and them. On your business pitch use the Social Process Model as a visual guide to explain everyone's contribution. The thing is, if you're managing work **remember** to manage it socially!

Now **move it!**

... move your work

... move your ecosystem

Socially!

About the Author

In case you were wondering

Elias Saad

linkedin.com/in/eliassaad

I'm here to help you work smarter. Where I find my best self is in designing solutions that evolve naturally in the work ecosystem.

As a business consultant I've assessed the Private and Social Return on Investment on more than 400 business projects and 30 state level programs, translating the result into actionable scorecards.

Understanding the big picture of work, with its tools and frameworks, has been easier with a BA in Finance & Accounting, a Post Graduate Degree in Project Appraisal and an MBA in Management and Innovation.

Working with people from Mexico, United States, United Kingdom, Latin America and China has helped me to appreciate the cultural similarities and differences of work processes and customs.

The Social Process Model is my contribution to the way we work. I will continue studying the social dimension, to better understand it, map it and manage it.

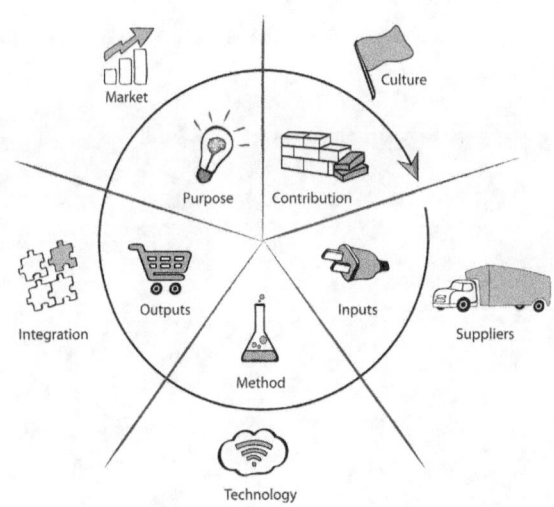

#workissocial

www.ingramcontent.com/pod-product-compliance
Lightning Source LLC
Chambersburg PA
CBHW070905180526
45168CB00005B/1934